RECIPES
from the
RALEIGH TAVERN BAKERY

Printed in the United States of America

Meals served to hungry travelers and local residents who patronized the Raleigh Tavern were prepared in a building on the site of the reconstructed kitchen and bakery. Servants carried the food across the courtyard into the tavern where most customers paid a fixed price for the meal of the day. Those meals consisted of readily available foods—meat or fish, vegetables and perhaps fruit, bread, and small beer. Tavern keepers also prepared special meals on demand.

Eighteenth-century diners enjoyed sweets just as we do today. Puddings, pies, jellies, cakes, and cookies—many similar to the baked goods offered for sale at the Raleigh Tavern Bakery—could all be found on colonial tables. Some original eighteenth-century recipes and modern adapted versions are presented here.

It can be fun—and educational—to experiment with recipes from long ago. Those who want to re-create the original colonial-era dishes, however, should be aware that recipes were very imprecise—witness the directions to add "a little white wine" or "a Piece of fresh butter" or to "set in an Oven not too hot." Some ingredients popular more than two hundred years ago are no longer considered edible. Ambergris, for example, a waxy substance from the intestines of the sperm whale, is frequently called for in colonial recipes. In addition, eighteenth-century tastes were different from ours today so that some dishes from that time taste bland or strange to modern palates.

The modern, adapted versions of these old recipes should hold fewer surprises for those who want to create in their own kitchens baked goods similar to those served in the eighteenth century.

Mary Miley Theobald

TO MAKE GINGER-BREAD CAKES

TAKE three pounds of flour, one pound of fugar, one pound of butter rubbed in very fine, two ounces of ginger beat fine, a large nutmeg grated; then take a pound of treacle, a quarter of a pint of cream, make them warm together, and make up the bread ftiff; roll it out, and make it up into thin cakes, cut them out with a tea-cup, or fmall glafs, or roll them round like nuts, and bake them on tin plates in a flack oven.

Hannah Glaffe, *The Art of Cookery, Made Plain and Eafy,* 7th ed. (London, 1760)

GINGERBREAD COOKIES
(50–60 cookies)

1 cup sugar
2 teaspoons ginger
1 teaspoon nutmeg
1 teaspoon cinnamon
½ teaspoon salt
1½ teaspoons baking soda
1 cup margarine, melted
½ cup evaporated milk
1 cup unsulfured molasses
¾ teaspoon vanilla extract (optional)
¾ teaspoon lemon extract (optional)
4 cups stone-ground or unbleached flour, unsifted

Combine the sugar, ginger, nutmeg, cinnamon, salt, and baking soda. Mix well. Add the melted margarine, evaporated milk, and molasses. Add the extracts if desired. Mix well. Add the flour 1 cup at a time, stirring constantly. The dough should be stiff enough to handle without sticking to fingers. Knead the dough for a smoother texture. Add up to ½ cup additional flour if necessary to prevent sticking. When the dough is smooth, roll it out ¼ inch thick on a floured surface and cut it into cookies. Bake on floured or greased cookie sheets in a preheated 375° F. oven for 10 to 12 minutes. The cookies are done if they spring back when touched.

APPLE PASTIES TO FRY

PARE and quarter Apples, and boil them in Sugar and Water, and a ſtick of cinamon, and when tender, put in a little white-wine, the juice of a lemon, a Piece of freſh butter, and a little ambergreaſe or orange-flower water; ſtir all together and when 'tis cold, put it in a Puff-paſte and fry them.

Paſte for Paſties

Rub ſix pounds of butter into fourteen pounds of flour; put to it eight eggs, whip the whites to ſnow and make it in a pretty ſtiff paſte with cold water.

E. Smith, *The Compleat Houſewife: or, Accompliſh'd Gentlewoman's Companion* (Williamſburg: Printed and ſold by William Parks, 1742)

APPLE TURNOVERS

Pastry
3 cups all-purpose flour
1 teaspoon salt
1 tablespoon sugar
1 cup shortening (up to $^1/_4$ of which may be butter)
1 egg, lightly beaten
$^1/_2$ cup very cold water

Combine the flour, salt, and sugar. Cut in the shortening with knives or a pastry blender until the mixture is mealy. Add the beaten egg and $^1/_4$ cup of water. Gradually add the remaining water if necessary to make a soft pastry. Chill well. Roll out the pastry $^1/_8$ inch thick on a floured surface. Cut 5-inch rounds of the pastry.

Apple Filling
7 to 8 tart pie apples, peeled and chopped
1 tablespoon lemon juice
$1^1/_4$ cups sugar
2 tablespoons flour
$^1/_2$ teaspoon cinnamon
$^1/_4$ teaspoon nutmeg
$^1/_4$ teaspoon cloves
$^1/_8$ teaspoon mace

Sprinkle the chopped apples with the lemon juice. Combine the sugar, flour, cinnamon, nutmeg, cloves, and mace. Mix well. Add the apples and mix gently until they are well coated. Place 2 tablespoons of filling on one half of each pastry circle. Moisten the edges with water and fold over to form a half round. Seal and crimp the edges with a fork. Brush the tops with cream or lightly beaten egg yolk. Sprinkle with sugar. Bake in a preheated 400° F. oven for 10 to 12 minutes. Apple turnovers may also be fried in deep hot fat (375° F.) until crisp and golden.

SALLY LUNN

BEAT four Eggs well; then melt a large Table-spoonful of Butter, put it in a Teacup of warm Water, and pour it to the Eggs with a Teaspoon of Salt and a Teacup of Yeaſt (this means Potato Yeaſt); beat in a Quart of Flour making the Batter ſtiff enough for a Spoon to ſtand in. Put it to riſe before the Fire the Night before. Beat it over in the Morning, greaſe your Cake-mould and put it in Time enough to riſe before baking. Should you want it for Supper, make it up at 10:00 o'Clock in the Morning in the Winter and 12: o'Clock in the Summer.

Recipe ca. 1770 of Governor Spotſwood's Grand-daughter from Charlotte Court Houſe, Virginia, reprinted in Helen Bullock, *The Williamſburg Art of Cookery* (Williamſburg, 1938)

SALLY LUNN

1 cup milk
¹/₂ cup shortening
4 cups sifted all-purpose flour, divided
¹/₃ cup sugar
2 teaspoons salt
2 packages active dry yeast
3 eggs

Grease a 10-inch tube cake pan or a bundt pan. Heat the milk, shortening, and ¼ cup of water until very warm—about 120° F. The shortening does not need to melt. Blend 1¹/₃ cups of flour with the sugar, salt, and dry yeast in a large mixing bowl. Blend the warm liquids into the flour mixture. Beat with an electric mixer at medium speed for about 2 minutes, scraping the sides of the bowl occasionally. Gradually add ²/₃ cup of the remaining flour and the eggs and beat at high speed for 2 minutes. Add the remaining flour and mix well. The batter will be thick but not stiff. Cover and let the dough rise in a warm, draft-free place (about 85° F.) until it doubles in bulk—about 1 hour and 15 minutes. Beat the dough down with a spatula or at the lowest speed on an electric mixer and turn into the prepared pan. Cover and let rise in a warm, draft-free place until it has increased in bulk one-third to one-half—about 30 minutes. Bake in a pre-heated 350° F. oven for 40 to 50 minutes. Run a knife around the center and outer edges of the bread and turn it onto a plate to cool.

TO MAKE PANCAKES

TAKE a pint of cream, and eight eggs, whites and all, a whole nutmeg grated, and a little falt; then melt a pound of rare difh butter, and a little fack; before you fry them, ftir it in: it muft be made as thick with three fpoonfuls of flour, as ordinary batter, and fry'd with butter in the pan, the firft Pancake, but no more: Strew fugar, garnifh with orange, turn it on the backfide of a plate.

E. Smith, *The Compleat Houfewife: or, Accomplifh'd Gentlewoman's Companion* (Williamfburg: Printed and fold by William Parks, 1742)

DESSERT CRÊPES
(8 servings)

1 cup all-purpose flour
1 tablespoon sugar
pinch of salt
3 eggs
1 1/2 cups milk
1 tablespoon brandy
2 tablespoons butter, melted
fruit, jam, or custard
whipped cream (optional)

Place the flour, sugar, and salt in the container of a food processor or blender. Turn the machine on and off quickly. Add the eggs, milk, and brandy and process for 1 minute. Scrape down the sides, add the melted butter, and process for 10 seconds longer. Strain the batter through a fine sieve. Refrigerate, covered, for 2 hours or overnight. Heat a crêpe pan to medium hot. Brush it lightly with butter. Swirling and tipping the pan, pour in just enough batter so that the bottom is entirely covered. Pour any excess batter back into the bowl. As soon as the top of the crêpe is covered with tiny holes, turn it over and cook for about 30 seconds on the other side. Stack the cooked crêpes between waxed paper. Fill the crêpes with fruit, jam, or custard. Roll and serve. Top with whipped cream if desired.

TO MAKE QUEEN CAKES

TAKE a pound of loaf-fugar, beat and fift it, a pound of flour well dried, a pound of butter, eight eggs, half a pound of currants wafhed and picked, grate a nutmeg, the fame quantity of mace and cinnamon, work your butter to a cream, then put in your fugar, beat the whites of your eggs near half an hour, mix them with your fugar and butter, then beat your yolks near half an hour, and put them to your butter, beat them exceedingly well together, then put in your flour, fpices, and the currants; when it is ready for the oven, bake them in tins, and duft a little fugar over them.

Hannah Glaffe, *The Art of Cookery, Made Plain and Eafy*, 7th ed. (London, 1760)

QUEEN'S CAKE

1 cup butter
1 cup sugar
5 eggs
1 teaspoon lemon extract
1 teaspoon orange extract
2 cups plus 1 tablespoon all-purpose flour
1/2 teaspoon baking powder
1/2 teaspoon cinnamon
2 cups currants

All of the ingredients should be at room temperature. Grease well and lightly flour a 9¼ x 5¼ x 2¾-inch loaf pan. Cream the butter and sugar. Add the eggs, 1 at a time, beating well after each addition. Add the lemon and orange extracts. Sift 2 cups of flour with the baking powder and cinnamon. Gradually add the flour mixture to the egg mixture. Dust the currants with the remaining 1 tablespoon of flour so they do not sink to the bottom of the mixture. Fold the currants into the mixture. Bake in a preheated 325° F. oven for 1 hour and 20 minutes or until done. Cool in the pan for 10 minutes before turning out onto a rack. Slice thinly.

APPLE PIE

A good cruft for great pies

TO a peck of flour the yolks of three eggs, then boil fome water, and put in half a pound of tried fewet, and a pound and half of butter. Skim off the butter and fewet, and as much of the liquor as will make a light good cruft; work it up well, and roll it out.

Hannah Glaffe, *The Art of Cookery, Made Plain and Eafy,* 7th ed. (London, 1760)

HAVING put a good puff pafte cruft round the edge of your difh, pare and quarter your apples, and take out the cores. Then lay a thick row of apples, and throw in half the fugar you intend to put into your pie. Mince a little lemon-peel fine, fpread it over the fugar and apples, and fqueeze a little lemon over them. Then fcatter a few cloves over it, and lay on the reft of your apples and fugar. Sweeten to your palate, and fqueeze a little more lemon. Boil the peeling of the apples and cores in fome fair water, with a blade of mace, till it has a pleafing tafte. Strain it, and boil the fyrup with a little fugar, till there be but a fmall quantity left. Then pour it into your pie, put on your upper cruft, and bake it. If you choofe it, you may put in a little quince or marmalade.

John Farley, *The London Art of Cookery, and Houfekeeper's Complete Affiftant,* 8th ed. (London, 1796)

APPLE PIE

Pastry
3 cups all-purpose flour
1 teaspoon salt
1 cup shortening (up to ¹/₄ of which may be butter)
1 egg, lightly beaten
¹/₂ cup very cold water

Combine the flour and salt. Cut in the shortening with knives or a pastry blender until the mixture is mealy. Add the beaten egg and ¹/₄ cup of water. Gradually add the remaining water if necessary to make a soft pastry. Chill well. Roll out the pastry ¹/₈ inch thick on a floured surface.

Apple Filling
7 to 8 tart apples, peeled and sliced
1 tablespoon lemon juice
³/₄ to 1 cup sugar
2 tablespoons flour
¹/₂ teaspoon cinnamon
¹/₄ teaspoon nutmeg
¹/₄ teaspoon cloves
¹/₈ teaspoon mace
1 to 2 tablespoons butter

Sprinkle the apple slices with the lemon juice. Combine the sugar, flour, cinnamon, nutmeg, cloves, and mace. Add the apple slices and mix gently until they are well coated. Fill the pastry-lined pie plate with the apple mixture. Dot with the butter. Add the top crust. Press the edges together firmly, flute, and slash vents in the center of the crust. Dust with sugar for sparkle if desired. Bake in a preheated 400° F. oven for 50 to 60 minutes or until the apples are done and the crust is golden brown.

✿✿✿

LEMON TART

A good cruſt for great pies

TO a peck of flour the yolks of three eggs; then boil ſome water, and put in half a pound of tried ſewet, and a pound and half of butter. Skim off the butter and ſewet, and as much of the liquor as will make a light good cruſt; work it up well, and roll it out.

Hannah Glaſſe, *The Art of Cookery, Made Plain and Eaſy,* 7th. ed. (London, 1760)

To make a Lemon Tart

TAKE three clear lemons, and grate off the outſide rinds; take the yolks of twelve eggs and ſix whites; beat them very well, ſqueeze in the juice of a lemon; then put in three quarters of a pound of fine powdered ſugar, and three quarters of a pound of freſh butter melted; ſtir all well together, put a ſheet of paſte at the bottom; and ſift ſugar on the top; put it in a briſk oven, three quarters of an hour will bake it: So ſerve it to the table.

E. Smith, *The Compleat Houſewife: or, Accompliſh'd Gentlewoman's Companion* (Williamſburg: Printed and ſold by William Parks, 1742)

LEMON PIE

Pastry
3 cups all-purpose flour
1 teaspoon salt
1 cup shortening (up to ¹/₄ of which may be butter)
1 egg, lightly beaten
¹/₂ cup very cold water

Combine the flour and salt. Cut in the shortening with knives or a pastry blender until the mixture is mealy. Add the beaten egg and ¹/₄ cup of water. Gradually add the remaining water if necessary to make a soft pastry. Chill well. Roll out the pastry ¹/₈ inch thick on a floured surface.

Lemon Filling
2 large lemons
1¹/₂ cups water
1 cup sugar
1 cup brown sugar
7 tablespoons cornstarch
¹/₄ teaspoon salt
3 egg yolks, lightly beaten
2 tablespoons butter
³/₄ cup raisins (optional)

Remove the peel from the lemons with a zester or with long, smooth, one-way strokes on a grater. Reserve. Remove as much of the white inner pith as possible. Slice the peeled lemons and remove any seeds. Process the lemon slices in a food processor for 1 minute or chop well. Cook the lemon pulp and reserved zest in 1¹/₂ cups of water for 8 to 10 minutes or until the zest is tender. Add the granulated sugar and simmer for 5 minutes or until the sugar is dissolved. Combine the brown sugar, cornstarch, and salt. Add the egg yolks and beat well to make a thick paste. Gradually add a little of the lemon mixture to the paste until the paste stirs fluidly. Pour the paste into the hot lemon mixture and cook over low heat, stirring constantly, until the mixture is thick and opaque. Remove from the heat. Add the butter and mix well. Add the raisins if desired. Cool until the mixture is lukewarm. Fill the pastry-lined pie plate with the lemon mixture. Add the top crust. Press the edges together firmly, flute, and slash vents in the center of the crust. Dust with sugar for sparkle if desired. Bake in a preheated 400° F. oven for 40 to 50 minutes or until the crust is golden brown.

OAT-MEAL CAKES

TAKE a peck of fine flour, half a peck of oatmeal, and mix it well together, put it to seven eggs well beat, three quarts of new milk, a little warm water, a pint of sack, and a pint of new yeast; mix all these well together, and let it stand to rise; then bake them. Butter the stone every time you lie on the cakes, and make them rather thicker than a pan-cake.

Elizabeth Moxon, *English Housewifery* (London, 1789)

OATMEAL COOKIES
(4 dozen)

1 cup shortening
1 cup sugar
2 eggs
$1/2$ cup molasses
$1/4$ cup milk
2 cups all-purpose flour
$1/2$ teaspoon salt
$1/2$ teaspoon baking soda
2 teaspoons cinnamon
1 teaspoon cloves
2 cups quick-cooking oats
$1/2$ cup raisins or currants (optional)

Cream the shortening and sugar. Add the eggs, molasses, and milk. Beat well. Sift the flour, salt, baking soda, cinnamon, and cloves together and add to the creamed mixture along with the quick-cooking oats. Add the raisins or currants if desired. Drop the mixture by heaping teaspoonfuls onto ungreased cookie sheets. Bake in a preheated 350° F. oven for 8 to 10 minutes or until brown but still soft.

INDIAN SLAPJACK

ONE quart of milk, 1 pint of indian meal, 4
eggs, 4 ſpoons of flour, little ſalt, beat together,
baked on gridles, or fry in a dry pan, or baked in
a pan which has been rub'd with ſuet, lard, or
butter.

Amelia Simmons, *American Cookery* (Hartford, 1796)

INDIAN CORN MUFFINS
(1¹/₂ dozen)

1 cup white cornmeal
1 cup all-purpose flour
1 teaspoon salt
3 teaspoons baking powder
2 tablespoons sugar
2 eggs, lightly beaten
1 cup milk
3 tablespoons butter, melted

Grease muffin tins that are 1¹/₂ inches in diameter. Sift the cornmeal, flour, salt, baking powder, and sugar into a mixing bowl. Combine the eggs, milk, and melted butter and add to the dry ingredients, mixing just until blended. Do not overmix. Spoon into the muffin tins, filling each tin completely full. Bake in a preheated 400° F. oven for 20 minutes or until done.

TO MAKE SHREWSBURY CAKES

TAKE two pounds of flour, a pound of fugar finely fearced, mix them together (take out a quarter of a pound to roll them in); take four eggs beat, four fpoonfuls of cream, and two fpoonfuls of rofe-water; beat them well together, and mix them with the flour into a pafte, roll them into thin cakes, and bake them in a quick oven.

Hannah Glaffe, *The Art of Cookery, Made Plain and Eafy*, 7th ed. (London, 1760)

SUGAR COOKIES
(3 dozen)

$1/4$ cup unsalted butter
$1/4$ cup shortening
1 cup sugar
$1^1/2$ teaspoons grated orange peel
1 teaspoon vanilla extract
1 egg
3 tablespoons milk
2 cups sifted all-purpose flour
1 teaspoon baking soda
$1/4$ teaspoon salt
2 teaspoons cream of tartar

Cream the butter, shortening, and sugar. Add the orange peel and vanilla extract. Add the egg and milk. Sift the flour, baking soda, salt, and cream of tartar and add to the creamed mixture. Mix well. Roll into 1-inch balls and roll the balls in sugar. Arrange the balls $1^1/2$ inches apart on ungreased cookie sheets. Flatten the balls gently with a small glass. Bake in a preheated 350° F. oven for 8 to 10 minutes or until very light golden brown.

PLUMB PYE

A good cruſt for great pies

TO a peck of flour the yolks of three eggs, then boil ſome water, and put in half a pound of tried ſewet, and a pound and half of butter. Skim off the butter and ſewet, and as much of the liquor as will make a light good cruſt; work it up well, and roll it out.

Hannah Glaſſe, *The Art of Cookery, Made Plain and Eaſy*, 7th ed. (London, 1760)

To make a cherry pie

MAKE a good cruſt, lay a little round the ſides of your diſh, throw ſugar at the bottom, and lay in your fruit and ſugar at top. A few red currants does well with them; put on your lid; and bake in ſlack oven.

MAKE a plumb pye the ſame way, and a gooſe-berry pye. If you would have it red, let it ſtand a good while in the oven, after the bread is drawn. A cuſtard is very good with the gooſe-berry pye.

Hannah Glaſſe, *The Art of Cookery, Made Plain and Eaſy*, 7th ed. (London, 1760)

PLUM TARTS
(8 tarts)

Pastry
3 cups all-purpose flour
1 teaspoon salt
1 cup shortening (up to $^1/_4$ of which may be butter)
1 egg, lightly beaten
$^1/_2$ cup very cold water

Combine the flour and salt. Cut in the shortening with knives or a pastry blender until the mixture is mealy. Add the beaten egg and ¼ cup of water. Gradually add the remaining water if necessary to make a soft pastry. Chill well. Lightly oil 8 individual tart pans. Roll out the pastry ⅛ inch thick on a floured surface. Line the tart pans with pastry.

Plum Filling
3 cups purple plums, pitted and sliced
2 tablespoons whipping cream
2 teaspoons plum jam or orange marmalade
$^1/_2$ cup sugar
1 tablespoon flour
2 teaspoons butter
$^1/_4$ teaspoon cinnamon
whipped cream (optional)

Arrange the sliced plums skin side down in the tart pans. Combine the whipping cream and jam and dot the plums with the mixture. Mix the sugar, flour, butter, and cinnamon until crumbly and spread the mixture over the plums. Bake in a preheated 375° F. oven for 30 minutes or until bubbly. Top with whipped cream if desired.

※※※

PEAR PYE

A good cruʃt for great pies

TO a peck of flour the yolks of three eggs, then boil ʃome water, and put in half a pound of tried ʃewet, and a pound and half of butter. Skim off the butter and ʃewet, and as much of the liquor as will make a light good cruʃt; work it up well, and roll it out.

Hannah Glaʃʃe, *The Art of Cookery, Made Plain and Eaʃy,* 7th ed. (London, 1760)

A BON CHRETIEN PEAR PYE
(Call'd a la Bonne Femme)

SLIT in two ʃome *bon chretien* Pears, take out the Core, pare them. Put into an earthen Pot ʃome of the Parings, put the Apple over them, add a Stick of Cinnamon and ʃome Sugar, and a Glaʃs of red Wine, with a little Water; and cover the Same with the Reʃt of the Parings. Cover your Pot with ʃome Paʃte round, and let your Pears be doing ʃlowly during five or ʃix Hours, with Fire under and over; then put ʃome Paʃte in the Bottom of a Baking-pan, as large as the dainty Diʃh you deʃign to ʃerve up, making round it a Cruʃt the Breadth of a Thumb; and let the Paʃte be not too thick. Put the Pan in the Oven, and when baked, glaze the Paʃte. Your Pears being done, place them in the Pan with their Liquor, which muʃt be of a lively red, ʃtrain it through a Sieve, and pour it over them. If your Liquor is too thin, ʃet it over again to thicken, then put it over your Pears. Serve it up either hot or cold.

Court & Country Confeƈtioner (London, 1770), reprinted in Helen Bullock, *The Williamʃburg Art of Cookery* (Williamʃburg, 1938)

※※※

PEAR PIE

Pastry
3 cups all-purpose flour
1 teaspoon salt
1 cup shortening (up to ¹/₄ of which may be butter)
1 egg, lightly beaten
¹/₂ cup very cold water

Combine the flour and salt. Cut in the shortening with knives or a pastry blender until the mixture is mealy. Add the beaten egg and ¼ cup of water. Gradually add the remaining water if necessary to make a soft pastry. Chill well. Roll out the pastry ⅛ inch thick on a floured surface.

Pear Filling
4 cups pears, peeled and sliced
1 tablespoon lemon juice
1 cup sugar
3 tablespoons flour
¹/₄ teaspoon nutmeg
pinch of salt
1 to 2 tablespoons butter

Sprinkle the pear slices with the lemon juice. Combine the sugar, flour, nutmeg, and salt. Mix well. Add the pear slices and mix gently until they are well coated. Fill the pastry-lined pie plate with the pear mixture. Dot with the butter. Add the top crust. Press the edges together firmly, flute, and slash vents in the center of the crust. Dust with sugar for sparkle if desired. Bake in a preheated 400° F. oven for 55 to 60 minutes or until the pears are done and the crust is golden brown.

PEACH TARTS

CHUSE a couple of Dozen of Peaches moderately ripe, and no way damaged, tear them open and take out the Stones.

Duſt ſome fine Sugar powdered over the Bottom of a Stewpan, lay the Peaches handſomely upon this, and ſet it over a gentle Fire; ſtir them carefully from Time to Time.

Make an under Cruſt with a Border of the Thickneſs of a Thumb; let this be baked; when the Diſh is ready with this Paſte, and the Peaches are done enough and are well coloured, turn them out of the Stewpan into the Diſh; pour a little boiling Water into the Stewpan and ſet it on the Fire again, this with the Sugar remaining about the Pan, will make a rich Syrup: Pour this over the Peaches in their Diſh, break the Stones, take out the Kernels carefully, and place them at Diſtances upon the Top of the Tart. This will be an exceeding elegant Diſh.

Martha Bradley, *The Britiſh Houſewife: or, the Cook, Houſekeeper's and Gardiner's Companion* (London, ca. 1770)

FRUIT TARTS
(8 tarts)

Pastry
3 cups all-purpose flour
1 teaspoon salt
1 tablespoon sugar
1 cup shortening (up to ¹/₄ of which may be butter)
1 egg, lightly beaten
¹/₂ cup very cold water
whipped cream (optional)

Combine the flour, salt, and sugar. Cut in the shortening with knives or a pastry blender until the mixture is mealy. Add the beaten egg and ¼ cup of water. Gradually add the remaining water if necessary to make a soft pastry. Chill well. Lightly oil 8 individual tart pans. Roll out the pastry ⅛ inch thick on a floured surface. Line the tart pans with the pastry. Prick the bottom and sides with a fork. Place waxed paper over the dough and fill the pans with dried beans to prevent the pastry from rising. Bake in a preheated 400° F. oven for 10 minutes. Remove from the oven, empty the beans, remove the waxed paper, prick the bottoms, and return to the oven for 5 minutes. Cool completely before filling.

Fruit Filling
1 cup red currant jelly
1 tablespoon sugar
1 teaspoon cherry brandy or kirsch
1 quart strawberries, raspberries, or blackberries or *8 fresh or canned peach halves*

Combine the red currant jelly and sugar in a small saucepan. Bring to a boil, stirring constantly. Remove from the heat. Add the cherry brandy or kirsch if desired. Cool completely. Spread a thin layer of the jelly mixture in the bottom of each tart shell. Arrange the fruit, stem ends or cut sides down, in the shells. Spoon the rest of the jelly mixture over the fruit. Garnish with whipped cream if desired.

NOTES

NOTES

NOTES

ISBN-13: 978-0-87935-106-9
ISBN-10: 0-87935-106-3